Wes & Judy Roberts & H. Norman Wright

After You Say "I DO"

HARVEST HOUSE PUBLISHERS

Eugene, Oregon 97402

After You Say "I Do"

Copyright © 1979 Harvest House Publishers
Eugene, Oregon 97402

Library of Congress Catalog Card Number: 79-66960
ISBN 0-89081-205-5

Contents

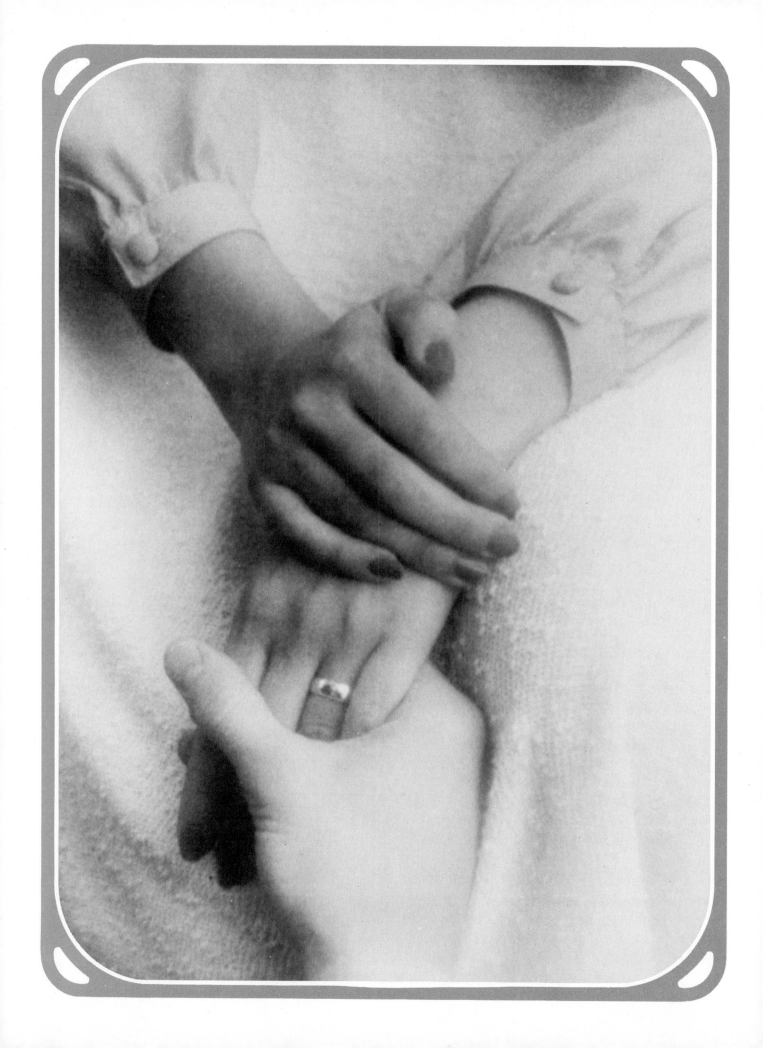

one

What Is Marriage?

Marriage is one of the most important facets of your life. Marriage contains unique and interesting potential. As one bright optimist put it, "Marriage is the only game of chance in town where both players can either win or both lose!" This manual has been developed to help you remove the risk element from your marriage. We trust that as you and your spouse work through this program, your present relationship will be strengthened and enriched to better insure an enriching, fulfilling, and growing marriage. We also hope that you will have a much more realistic perception of yourself, your spouse, and your marriage.

First of all, let's relive part of your courtship.

1.   When did you meet? Describe this as well as you can remember.

2.   Who first wanted to date?

3.   What did you like about the other person right at first?

4.   When did you decide on the inside "you're for me"?

5.   Who was the first person you told that you were engaged?

6.   In what way is your spouse different than and similar to your parents?

7.   Define marriage. What is its purpose?

8.   How does your marriage relationship agree or differ from this definition and purpose?

9.   Do you believe that marriage is a contract? Why or why not?

10. How do you think your spouse would answer these questions?

11. Read the following quotations. After you have read each of them indicate which portions you agree with and which portions you disagree with.

"Marriage resembles a pair of shears, so joined that they cannot be separated; often moving in opposite directions, yet always punishing anyone who comes between them."[1]

"Is marriage a private action of two persons in love, or a public act of two pledging a contract? Neither, it is something other. Very much other! Basically, the Christian view of marriage is not that it is primarily or essentially a binding legal and social contract. The Christian understands marriage as a covenant made under God and in the presence of fellow members of the Christian family. Such a pledge endures, not because of the force of law or the fear of its sanctions, but because an unconditional covenant has been made. A covenant more solemn, more binding, more permanent than any legal contract."[2]

"A system by means of which persons who are sinful and contentious are so caught up by a dream and a purpose bigger than themselves that they work through the years, in spite of repeated disappointment, to make the dream come true."[3]

"...Marriage is a relationship between man and woman intended by God to be a monogamous relationship, intended to be a permanent bond in which many needs are satisfied—the need to love and be loved, the need for deep friendship, for sharing, for companionship, for sexual satisfaction, for children, the need to escape loneliness. Marriage ought to be a bond of love, reflecting the love Christ has for His people, a bond of sacrificial love where husband and wife have become one, one flesh, a unity."[4]

Genesis 2:18-25

1.   Who originated the marriage institution?

2.   What are the purposes of marriage and why was it originated? (*See Genesis 1:28; 2:18; Ephesians 5:22-32.*)

(1)

(2)

(3)

(4)

3.   How is marriage good? (*Genesis 2:18; Hebrews 13:4.*)

4.   What is a helpmeet, in your opinion? In your spouse's opinion?

5.   What does leaving mother and father involve?

6.   What do the words "shall cleave" mean?

7.   What do the words "they shall be one flesh" mean to you?

8.   List six behaviors that you presently perform in marriage to promote and maintain the oneness characteristic of marriage.

(1)

(2)

(3)

(4)

(5)

(6)

9.   List three of the most important Scripture verses upon which you would like to base your continuing marriage relationship. (Please use passages other than *Ephesians 5:21-33; 1 Corinthians 13;* and *1 Peter 3* as most couples automatically look to these. They are important, but think through other important passages that will assist you in establishing the type of marriage you are seeking.)

(1)

(2)

(3)

Here is another definition of marriage that you may want to consider. The marriage relationship is a school, a learning and growing environment in which (if everything is as it should be) both partners can grow and develop. The relationship grows along with them. If you can see marriage as an opportunity for growth, you can be satisfied and can satisfy your spouse.

Dr. David Hubbard graphically described the marriage relationship when he said, "Marriage does not demand perfection. But it must be given priority. It is an institution for sinners. No one else need apply. But it finds its finest glory when sinners see it as God's way of leading us through his ultimate curriculum of love and righteousness."[5] Have you ever thought about the purpose of marriage in that light before?

Here's another definition of marriage which Norm Wright has developed over the years. Consider it carefully, and then talk over your feelings with your partner: "A Christian marriage is a total commitment of two people to the person of Jesus Christ and to each other. It is a commitment in which there is no holding back of anything. Marriage is a pledge of mutual fidelity, it is a partnership of mutual subordination. A Christian marriage is similar to a solvent, a freeing up of the man and woman to be themselves and become all that

God intends for them to become. Marriage is a refining process that God will use to have us become the man or woman He wants us to become."

Think about it. God will use your marriage for His purpose. He will mold and refine you for your own benefit and for His glory.

You may be thinking that in your marriage there are only two individuals involved. That is true, but there is a third party who can give even a greater meaning to your individual and married life—that person is Jesus Christ. In what way will you allow the presence of Jesus Christ in your life to make a difference in your marriage?

Read *Matthew 7:24-27.* This passage is talking about building your house upon a firm foundation. List what you believe are ten firm foundations which will go into making a solid marriage relationship.

1.

2.

3.

4.

5.

6.

7.

8.

9.

10.

Reasons for Marriage

There are many reasons and motivating factors for marriage. What are yours? Have you ever thought about them? Here are two very important questions for you to answer and then discuss with your spouse.

1. What are you receiving out of marriage that you wouldn't have received by remaining single?

2. On a separate piece of paper, list the reasons why you married your spouse. After you have done that, list the reasons why you think your spouse married you. Then share the results.

Now compare your reasons for marriage with the following list which has been compiled by several specialists in marriage and family life education. These are unhealthy reasons for marriage! If you find that any of these appear either on your list or in your own mind, you should spend time discussing them with your spouse or your minister.

1. To spite or get back at your parents.
2. Because of a negative self-image—you thought marriage would make you feel worthwhile and would give meaning to your life.
3. To be a therapist or counselor to your spouse.
4. Fear of being left out! Being left as a bachelor or an old maid!
5. Fear of independence.
6. Married on the rebound—you were hurt in a former love relationship and to ease your hurt you immediately choose another.
7. Fear of hurting the other person—you were afraid of what would have happened to your spouse if you broke up even though you knew that marriage was not the answer.
8. To escape an unhappy home.
9. Because you were pregnant or your spouse was pregnant.
10. Because you had sex.

A few of the positive reasons for marriage:

1. Companionship.
2. To work together and fulfill your own and each other's needs.

3. To fulfill sexual needs in the way God intends.
4. Love (by love is meant an adequate blending of the various types of love as explained in chapter 3).
5. Because you were convinced that it was God's will for you to marry this person.

Evaluate your ''marriageability'' by examining the personality traits of yourself and your spouse. List eight character or personality traits that you feel have helped your marriage.

1.

2.

3.

4.

5.

6.

7.

8.

Turn in your Bible to *Galatians 5:22,23* and read over the fruit of the Spirit. Would these traits, manifested in a person, give him a greater potential of success in marriage? If so, indicate which of these you manifest and which of them you are still having difficulty displaying.

In addition to utilizing the fruit of the Spirit as a guide for evaluating a marriage, eight marriageability traits have been isolated which give a person a greater possibility of having an enriched and satisfying marriage:

1. Adaptability and flexibility—the ability to change and adapt.
2. Empathy—the ability to be sensitive to the needs, hurts, and desires of others, to feel with them and experience the world from their perspective.
3. The ability to work through problems.
4. The ability to give and receive love.
5. Emotional stability—accepting one's emotions and controlling them.
6. Communication.
7. Similarities between the couple themselves.
8. Similar family background.

The natural inclination is to look at this list and say, "Oh yes, that's us. We are like that and have these characteristics." If you feel these traits are present, give a specific example of how each of the first six traits was manifested in the past two week. Then, for traits 7 and 8, give examples of the similarity for each one.

1.

2.

3.

4.

5.

6.

7. (1) _____
   (2) _____
   (3) _____
   (4) _____
   (5) _____

8. (1) _____
   (2) _____
   (3) _____
   (4) _____
   (5) _____

VALUES IN MARRIAGE

The values and meanings each of us attach to marriage are greatly influenced by our parents and their ideas. Some of us imitate our parents closely, with values passed on from generation to generation. Others move far from the parental example, rejecting the "tried and true" values and searching for new marriage designs. Because parents of a married couple have had different values, husband and wife may expect different things from marriage. It is wise to take time to find out what is important to each partner. In that way, the marriage can be designed to meet the needs and expectations of both husband and wife.

THE IDEAL MARRIAGE

Wife's Thoughts	Husband's Thoughts

Ten years ago, how would you have described the ideal marriage?

What is an ideal marriage for you now?

If your ideas have changed, what were the causes?

Any predictions about the ideal marriage of the future? What will your marriage be like in ten years? What will your child's marriage be like?

On a separate sheet of paper, list—both you and your spouse—as many values as you can that are important to you in marriage. Try to get 20 items if you can.

Next, circle the 5 items that are the most important to you . Have your partner do the same on his/her list.

Now list some things you think are important to your partner in marriage. Put a star by those items that are also on your list.

Share your list with your partner. Are the lists similar? Did you express the same ideas in different ways? Did you accurately predict what is important to your partner? (When predictions were wrong, what had made you think that way?)

Because people change continually, the design of marriage may need to be changed from time to time. How would the changed list below effect the five values you named as being most important to you in marriage?

a. You moved in with your parents.
b. You moved 1,000 miles away from all relatives.
c. The major wage earner becomes unemployed with little hope for future employment.
d. You adopt a new baby.
e. You were suddenly childless with no hope of more children.
f. Husband and wife took jobs in different towns, establishing two separate homes.
g. You both retired on one-third of your current income.
h. You discovered that one partner had just six months to live.

two

Uniqueness and Acceptance in Marriage

Your partner is not you. He or she is other, created in God's image, not yours. He has a right to be other, to be treated and respected as other.

"Before you married you probably had a preconceived fantasy of your ideal mate or the perfect marriage. After a while you began to realize that your fantasy and the person you have married diverge sharply. At that point you may have embarked upon a reform program, forgetting that only God can make a tree. You misconstrued the words of the wedding ceremony 'and the two shall become one' to mean that your mate should become like you and your fantasy. You would become one in likes, preferences, interests, hobbies, ideas, even reactions and feelings: YOURS! The oneness in marriage is not similarity or sameness in matters relating to ideas or feelings but to the oneness of understanding. Any attempt to mold our mates in an effort to match them to our fantasies is arrogance on our part and an insult to them. While it is true that we can never mold or remake another person, we can 'allow' them to change."

The instruction on right living in *Ephesians 4:2* can be applied to the marriage relationship. "Living as becomes you—with complete lowliness of mind (humility) and meekness (unselfishness, gentleness, mildness), with patience, bearing with one another and making allowances because you love one another" (*Amplified*). Look at the last part of the verse: "making allowances because you love one another." List six specific examples of how this portion could be applied in your marriage relationship. Try to think of these in relation to your differentness.

1.

2.

3.

4.

5.

6.

Complete the next section of your workbook.

SIMILARITIES How are my spouse and I similar?	DIFFERENCES How are my spouse and I different?	EFFECT How can these differences or similarities complement or help one another in our marriage?

Which of the differences have you thanked God for?

Differences in Marriage—The Potential for Growth and Enhancement

Every person who marries has characteristics similar to the one he marries. But he also has many that are different. Different ways of perceiving, thinking, feeling, and behaving are part of marital adjustment. Differentness is important because it holds out the promise of need fulfillment for each person. It is important to remember that one of the main motivating factors toward marriage is the person's need to feel complete because of what the other person has to offer. Consciously or unconsciously people choose others who can help them feel complete. On the other hand this innate differentness contains the seeds for hurt and disruption. Why? The answer is quite simple. We are threatened by the differences in our spouse. We are afraid that we might have to adjust our way

of thinking and doing things. We also believe that "If it's different, it's wrong!" Many problems occur because of the lack of tolerance for differences of attitude or opinions in the marital relationship. Problems occur because we do not allow the other person to be different. But consider these thoughts:

"In the midst of the marital struggle the honeymoon dream vanishes, and the despair over the old relationship comes up for reexamination. Suddenly each spouse turns his eyes away from the partner, and looks inwardly and asks 'What am I doing to my partner? What is wrong with me? What am I misunderstanding? What must I do to rescue this marriage?' If honestly asked the answers are not far behind: 'I really married my wife because of her difference. It is not my job to make her over, but rather to discover and to value that difference. But before I can do that I must accept my difference and I really need her to help me discover my uniqueness. My task is not to mold her into a beautiful vase, but to

13

participate with her to discover that beautiful vase even as we discover it in me. How arrogant of me to think I could shape another human being! How humble it makes me to realize that I need to yield to another and thereby be changed! Our relationship will change both of us—in a process of being shaped into a form far more beautiful than either could imagine.' "

"We try to change people to conform to our ideas of how they should be. So does God. But there the similarity ends. Our ideas of what the other person should do or how he should act may be an improvement or an imprisonment. We may be setting the other person free of behavior patterns that are restricting his development, or we may be simply chaining him up in another behavioral bondage."[8]

1. If you are definitely bothered by the uniqueness of your spouse ask yourself, "What would it be like being married to a person just like me—and would I like it?"

2. In what way will the presence of Jesus Christ in your life help you adjust to differences in your marriage?

three

Love as a Basis for Marriage

Most couples say they are married because they love their spouse. Let's assume that in this society in order to be married you had to convince a jury in a court of law that you really did love the other person. Write in detail the facts you would present to a jury. Include in your presentation your own definition of love.

What is love? What does the world think love is? Here are several definitions. Which of these do you agree with?

"Love is a feeling you feel when you get a feeling that you've never felt before."

"Love is a perpetual state of anesthesia."

"Love is a find, a fire, a heaven, a hell—where pleasure, pain, and sad repentance dwell !"

"Love is a grave mental disease."

"To love somebody is not just a strong feeling—it is a decision, it is a judgment, it is a promise."

"Love is an unconditional commitment to an imperfect person."

What does the Word of God say about love? Look up some of the following passages of scripture to discover love from God's perspective. We'd suggest using a modern translation. What is the central thought or example in each passage?

THE BIBLICAL
CONCEPT OF LOVE

1. *Proverbs 17:17* _____

2. *Matthew 6:24* _____

3. *Matthew 22:37-39* _____

4. *Luke 6:27-35* _____

5. *Luke 10:25-37* _____

6. *John 3:16* _____

7. *John 13:34* _____

8. *Romans 13:8-10* _____

9. *Romans 14:15* _____

10. *1 Corinthians 8:1* _____

11. *Galatians 2:20* _____

12. *Galatians 5:13* _____

13. *Galatians 6:2* _____

14. *Ephesians 4:2* _____

15. *Ephesians 5:2* _____

16. *Ephesians 5:25* _____

17. *Titus 2:3-5* _____

18. *1 Peter 4:8* _____

19. *1 John 3:16-18* _____

1 Corinthians 13:4-7 gives the Bible's definition of love. These verses indicate that love consists of many elements—negative and positive. As you consider them below, give three creative examples of how each could be applied in your marriage. Be specific.

1. Suffers long—endures offenses, is not hasty, waits for the Lord to right all wrong.

(1)

(2)

(3)

2. Is kind—not inconsiderate, seeks to help, is constructive, blesses when cursed, helps when hurt, demonstrates tenderness.

(1)

(2)

(3)

3. Is not envious but content—is not jealous of another person's success or competition.

(1)

(2)

(3)

4. Is not arrogant, but humble—is not haughty, but lowly and gracious.

(1)

(2)

(3)

5. Is not boastful, but reserved—does not show off, try to impress, want to be the center of attraction.

(1)

(2)

(3)

6. Is not rude, but courteous.

(1)

(2)

(3)

7. Is not selfish, but self-forgetful.

(1)

(2)

(3)

8. Is not irritable, but good tempered.

(1)

(2)

(3)

9. Is not vindictive or wrathful, but generous.

(1)

(2)

(3)

10. Does not delight in bringing another person's sins to light, but rejoices when another person obeys the truth.

(1)

(2)

(3)

11. Is not rebellious, but brave, conceals rather than exposes another person's wrongdoing to others.

(1)

(2)

(3)

12. Is not suspicious but trustful, not cynical, makes every allowance, looks for an explanation that will show the best in others.

(1)

(2)

(3)

13. Is not despondent, but hopeful, does not give up because it has been deceived or denied.

(1)

(2)

(3)

14. Is not conquerable, but invincible—can outlast problems.

(1)

(2)

(3)

How would you resolve this conflict?

After eight years of marriage Ken tells a marriage counselor that he no longer has any feeling for his wife. "It isn't like when we were first married," he says, "I knew without a doubt I loved her then. I had strong emotional feelings that were unmistakable. Now that is all gone. I admire her. She is a wonderful girl, a good wife and mother. I'm really more attracted to a girl I used to date in high school." Sandy is frustrated over the whole matter. She says she loves her husband and children and wants to hold her family together. Neither wants a divorce. *"How can I regain that feeling for my wife?"* he asks. *"Was it something I did to destroy his love for me?"* she asks.

1. What are the causes of the problem?

Sandy

Ken

2. What should they do to resolve the problem?

Sandy

Ken

3. What suggestions does *Revelation 2:1-5* give on how to fall in love again?

(1)

(2)

(3)

Your Marriage Needs Three Types of Love
eros, philia, agape

Eros is the love that seeks sensual expression. Eros is a romantic love, sexual love. It is inspired by the biological structure of human nature. The husband and wife, in a good marriage, will love each other romantically and erotically.

In a good marriage the husband and wife are also friends. Friendship means companionship, communication, and cooperation. This is known as philia.

Agape is self-giving love, gift love, the love that goes on loving even when the other becomes unlovable. *Agape love is not just something that happens to you; it's something you make happen.* Love is a personal act of commitment. Christ's love (and hence the pattern for our love) is gift love. Christ's love for us is a sacrificial love. Christ's love is unconditional. Christ's

love is an eternal love. Agape is kindness. It is being sympathetic, thoughtful, and sensitive to the needs of your loved one. Agape is contentment and agape love is forgiving love.

If individuals would put forth effort purposely to increase philia and agape love, all three types of love would increase. The friendship love of philia can enhance and enrich both of the others. The agape love in turn can increase and enhance the others. Both agape and philia can enrich the eros love so it does not have to diminish as much as it usually does. It too can flourish if properly nurtured, and if so, the other types of love are reinforced. But all three must be given conscious effort.

In your marriage what can you do to demonstrate these three kinds of love? Under each word write five specific examples of what you will do to enhance your love relationship.

EROS	PHILIA	AGAPE
1.		
2.		
3.		
4.		
5.		

What do you feel are the three main hindrances in a couple's marriage to developing love and continuing to grow?

1.

2.

3.

Your love will either live or die. What kills love? Love dies when you spend little or no time together and when you stop sharing activities that are mutually enjoyable. Love is created or destroyed by pairing or failing to pair the partner with pleasurable activities over a period of time. Love dies from failure on the part of both individuals to reinforce appropriate behavior in each other. Smiling, caressing, complimenting, showing compassion, and spending time together are behaviors in marriage that may not be reinforced. If they are not reinforced they may disappear. If your partner stops doing things that you like, your love feelings may disappear.

1. What do you do now to reinforce the behaviors from your spouse that you enjoy?

2. Without asking your spouse, what behaviors does he/she enjoy from you?

3. How will the presence of Jesus Christ in your life help you to love your spouse through eros, philia, and agape love?

four

What Did You Expect from Marriage?

Every person who marries enters the marriage relationship with certain expectations. These expectations come from many sources such as parents, values, society, books, speakers, our own ideas, etc. It is very important to take the time to find out what these expectations were and are, which can be achieved, which are realistic, and how to handle them when things do not go according to plans. The word *expectation* carries with it the attitude of hope. Hope has been defined as "the anticipation of something good." Hope is necessary as it motivates us and often keeps us going.

The next exercise will take some thought and time on your part. Write ten expectations you have of your spouse. These can be simple or elaborate. For example, a husband might expect his wife to be at the door when he arrives home, always to be at home and never work, and to have sex with him whenever he wants it. A wife might expect her husband to go to her parents' house with her whenever she goes, to be the spiritual leader in their home, and to spend Saturdays at home and not out hunting.

List your expectations now, but do not discuss them with your partner yet. You will be using the columns on the right later.

	C	S	N
1.			
2.			
3.			
4.			
5.			
6.			
7.			
8.			
9.			
10.			
11.			
12.			
13.			
14.			
15.			
16.			
17.			
18.			
19.			
20.			

Now list ten expectations you think your partner has for you in marriage.

1.

2.

3.

4.

5.

6.

7.

8.

9.

10.

Let's briefly talk about disappointment. We all experience disappointments because some of our expectations, hopes and dreams are not realized. List three of the most disappointing experiences of your life and then indicate what you did or how you handled the disappointment.

1.

2.

3.

Now let's go back to your twenty expectations of your spouse. Take each expectation and, on a separate piece of paper, write one or two sentences indicating how your marriage relationship is affected if this expectation isn't met.

Now, take your list of twenty expectations and share your list with your partner. Take your partners list and read it to yourself. As you read each one of your partner's expectations of you, place a check mark under the appropriate column. **C** stands for "cinch." You feel that the expectation you have just read is a cinch to fulfill. **S** stands for "sweat." It takes some hard work and sweat but it can be done. **N** stands for "no way." You feel that the expectation is impossible. When the two of you have completed your evaluation of the expectations, give them back and then spend some time discussing them.

(If you have the tape series "Enriching Your Marriage" available, you may want to play the tape by Wes Roberts and hear his presentation on expectations and the experience of his own marriage.)

There are three very common expectations that couples have for their marriage. Couples expect their marriage to work out and never end in divorce. This is an excellent goal, but what can be done to make it a reality? Write a paragraph indicating what you personally are doing to make your marriage work. When you and your spouse have done this, share your paragraphs together.

Another expectation couples have is fidelity. They expect that they will be faithful to each other. After all, infidelity as commonly conceived would be out of the question in a Christian marriage. Fidelity, however, concerns not only sexual faithfulness, but other areas of faithfulness as well. For example, some spouses are unfaithful to their mate through their work. The center of attention, which belongs to their spouse, is given to their job. Some spouses are unfaithful to their mate through their mothers, fishing trips, golf, cars, church work, housekeeping, children, etc. You see, by putting any other person, possession, or activity (with the exception of your relationship with Jesus Christ) before your spouse, you could be unfaithful to the marriage relationship. What we need in marriage is creative fidelity. This means being sensitive to the needs of each other, supporting your partner, and being with him emotionally and physically.

Couples also expect their marriage to progress smoothly onward and upward without any major upheavals or adjustments. Consider the following suggested outline of the three stages of marriage.

**The Three Stages of Marriage
(and some words and ideas
that go with these stages)[9]**

	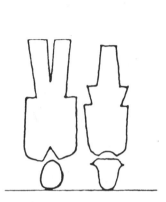	
Enchantment	*Disenchantment*	*Maturity*
On Cloud 9	Upset	Feet on the ground
Perfect	Terrible	I need you
Just right	Absolutely wrong	How do you see it?
Forever	I quit	Let's work it out
Infatuated	Hurt	I'll help you
Idolize	Put down	Encourage
Numb	Splintered	Whole
Fascinated	Irritated	Refreshed
Charmed	Wretched	Thankful
Captivated	Burdened	Free
Ecstasy	Uncomfortable	Comfortable
Thrilled	Bitter	Friendly
Preoccupied	Trapped	Growing
We've arrived	We'll never make it	Together, we can make it

It has been suggested that couples go through these three stages. What about you? Perhaps in your own relationship you have experienced some of the words in the various stages already. Circle any of the words in the three stages which indicate how you have felt at one time or another in your marriage. Then underline the words which describe your current state. When you have finished writing, then share your responses together.

Often many of our expectations come from our own home and our own background. Complete the following statements and then share your responses with your partner.

1.   This is what you need to know about my family life as I was growing up in order to understand me:

2. If I could have changed one thing about my family life as I was growing up, it would have been...

3. Because I want or don't want this to occur in my own marriage and family life I am...

4. My parents have influenced my attitudes about marriage by...

5. Something from my parents' marriage that I want to have in mine is...

6. Something from my parents' marriage that I prefer not having in mine is...

7. Talk with your partner and list, on a separate piece of paper, ten similarities and ten differences about his home and family life and yours. Discuss these together. How are any of these affecting your own marriage?

Change in marriage will happen. How will you adjust to it? Did you realize that even positive changes can disrupt a marriage relationship? A person who is married to a non-Christian and has prayed for many years for the spouse to accept the Lord suddenly discovers that his spouse has now accepted the Lord and has completely changed his life-style. This upsets the Christian spouse. Why? An alcoholic man suddenly stops drinking and changes his life-style, which is what his wife has been asking for, but now she is upset. Why? A passive, submissive husband begins to assert himself in a positive way and becomes involved with the family and the children. His wife is a bit upset. Why?

Even though certain undesirable behaviors are occurring in a marriage relationship, the couple learns to adjust to them. But when one makes a positive change, it upsets the equilibrium and the spouse who has been asking for the change discovers that he (or she) must now, himself, change. He must learn to adapt to the new person, which could be a bit uncomfortable. What he has been complaining about is no longer there, and now he must face himself and his own attitude and learn how to relate to this new person.

The one spouse may ask, "If he could change now, why did he wait so long and put me through all of this?" You might keep this in mind when you ask for change. Remember this: The best way to help another to change is to make changes in your own life. The other person *may* change as he learns to relate to the new you!

Write how you would react to the following circumstances which could cause changes in your own marriage:

1. a miscarriage

2. death of a child

3. major financial difficulty

4. being fired from a job

5. wife working instead of the husband

6. major personal illness

7. being involved in a major lawsuit of potentially great financial loss and severe emotional stress

8. living in an apartment instead of the home you were in for five years

9. living in the country instead of the city

10. husband quitting his job to go into business for himself

11. wife wanting to go to work while leaving three children at home

12. child does not turn out the way you wanted

13. two more children than you planned on having

Look back at *James 1:2,3*. The word *count* or *consider* means "an internal attitude of heart and mind that causes the trial and circumstance of life to affect a person either adversely or beneficially." The verse tense used here means that this is a decisiveness of action, not just a passive giving up or resignation. Another interpretation of this word could be "make up your mind to regard adversities as something to welcome or be glad about." It is an attitude of the mind.

The word *trials* means "outward trouble or stress, or disappointments, sorrow, or hardships." These are situations that you had no part in bringing about. They are not sin. They just happened. They are all of the various sorts of trouble that we have in our human life.

The word *endurance* or *patience* as it is sometimes translated means "fortitude" or "the quality of being stabilized or remaining alive." It is, in a sense, a picture of standing firm under pressure rather than trying to escape.

How will the presence of Jesus Christ in your life help you to fulfill your expectations of marriage and accept the ones that are not fulfilled?

(Note: For additional study on the effect of change see *"How to Cope With Conflict, Crisis and Change"* by Dr. Lloyd Ahlem; Regal Books)

five

Goals in Marriage

Less than three percent of married couples have set goals for their marriage. Goals are vital, for unless you have something in mind that you want to work toward or achieve, you will not get very far. What goals do you have for your marriage? What do you want your marriage to become? What do you want it to reflect? What do you want from your marriage?

We all want to be happy in our marriage relationship, but that is such a broad goal and it needs to be made more specific. For a goal to be a good goal, it must have 3 characteristics: 1) It must be specific (well-defined, to the point); 2) It must be realistic and/or attainable; 3) It must have a time limit (next week, this summer, in 20 years —someday does not count).

You might also think in terms of the various aspects of your relationship: intellectual, physical, emotional, spiritual, social, financial. What goals would you like to achieve in each of these areas?

List eight goals for your marriage on the goal wheel below. Write one goal in each of six spaces. Then take one of the remaining spaces and write a goal that you yourself would like to achieve within three to five years. In the remaining space write a goal that you would like to see your spouse achieve within three to five years. Remember, a goal should be specific, realistic, attainable, and have a time limit.

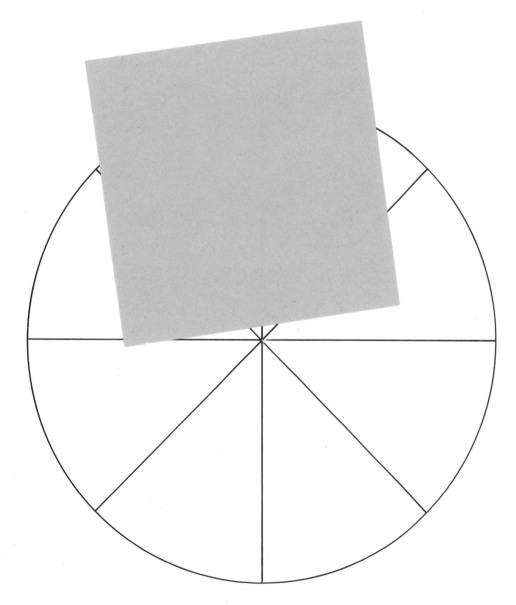

Now follow these directions concerning your goals.

1.   Place an asterisk(*) by four of the eight goals that you feel are the most important. Then rank them in order of importance.

2.   Place a *0* by any two of the eight goals that you would be willing to forego if absolutely necessary.

3.   Place a *$* by the ones that cost money.

4.   Place a *P* by the ones you learned from your parents.

5.   Place an *S* by the ones you think your spouse wrote down. Give a one-sentence explanation why your marriage goals are important to the health of your marriage.

6.   Now share and discuss your goals with your spouse.

7.   Having goals is great—scary but great! But now the good work begins. Look at your goals as statements of faith in God. "We can make our plans, but the final outcome is in God's hands. — commit your work to to the Lord, then it will succeed" (Proverbs 16:1, 3; Living Bible). "Live life then, with a due sense of responsibility, not as men and women who do not know the meaning and purpose of life, but as those who do" (Ephesians 5:15-16, Phillips). A goal is a statement about how we hope things are going to be in the future. Now, select two of your marriage goals which are the most similar and develop a plan to reach them. You will need to take some mini-steps to reach the longer goal you listed. Remember that these short term goals still need those three characteristics which make a goal a good one! It is important to periodically evaluate and determine goals because goals do change.

8.   How will the presence of Jesus Christ in your life assist you in setting and achieving your goals?

six

Fulfilling Needs in Marriage

One of the motivating factors for marriage is the fulfillment of needs in one's life. It is admirable to say that we are marrying the other person in order to help him fulfill his needs; but, to be very honest, we do hope and believe that our needs will be met too. In marriage counseling we find that one of the major complaints couples bring in is that of not having their needs met. Often one partner is attempting to meet the needs of the other, but he doesn't always know what the needs are and /or doesn't know exactly how to meet them.

Thus we feel that it is important for a married person to define his needs specifically and then indicate how he would like his partner to respond in order to meet those needs. Some have asked, ''Doesn't it take the romance out of marriage if you have to tell the other person exactly what you need?'' Not really. In fact it can increase the romance as now your spouse won't have to play the game of mind reading and try to figure out what you need and what you want!

Let's take a look at your needs. Write specifically what you think your needs are for each of the four areas below. Then indicate what your spouse can do to fulfill those needs.

NEEDS IN MARRIAGE	WHAT MY SPOUSE CAN DO TO FULFILL THESE NEEDS
Physical:	
Emotional:	
Spiritual:	
Social and intellectual:	

Now exchange your workbook with your partner but cover up the section that shows what you would like your spouse to do to meet your needs. Read over each other's needs and then, on a separate piece of paper, write what you think you can do to meet his needs. When you have completed this assignment, reveal the covered portion and discover how perceptive you are in deciding how to meet the other's needs!

Years ago a psychologist named Abraham Maslow suggested that each person has certain basic needs in his or her life. He listed these needs in order of importance. First, a person seeks to fulfill his physiological needs. These are those things that are necessary in order to sustain life: food, water, oxygen, rest, etc. Second, a person seeks to fulfill safety needs, which involve the need for a safe environment, protection from harm, etc. Third, after having the first two sets of needs fulfilled, a person seeks to fulfill his or her need for love and belonging. This includes a desire for affectionate relationships with others. Fourth, a person seeks to fulfill his or her need for esteem. Esteem involves receiving recognition as a worthwhile person. Finally, after the other levels of needs are met, a person seeks to fulfill the need of self-actualization. This is the need to become the person one has the potential to become, to develop into a full, creative person.

MASLOW'S LEVELS OF NEEDS

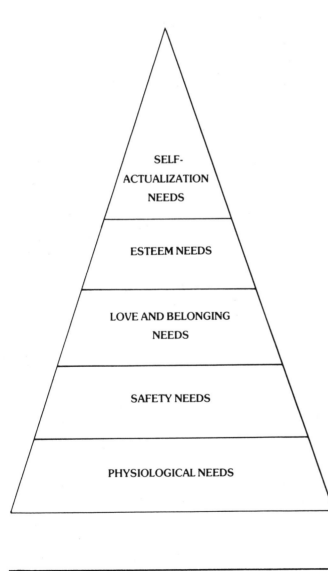

SELF-ACTUALIZATION NEEDS

ESTEEM NEEDS

LOVE AND BELONGING NEEDS

SAFETY NEEDS

PHYSIOLOGICAL NEEDS

Most husbands and wives help to fulfill the first two levels of needs in each other—the physiological and safety needs. Most husbands, for example, allow their wives enough air, water, food, and rest. And most are concerned about keeping the car in good running order, making sure the house is safe with proper lighting, ventilation, locks, and so on. But where most husbands and wives fall down is in meeting their spouse's needs for love and belonging, esteem, and self-actualization.

Looking at the chart of the hierarchy of needs, complete these sentences:

1.   During our marriage I will try to meet the needs of my partner in the last three areas by...

2.   My partner can best meet my own needs for love, esteem and self-actualization by...

Now take your Bible and look for passages that claim that God has promised to meet every need on your list. Instead of relying on ourself or our spouse to meet this need, we find that God has promises for us which will give us the stability we are seeking. You may want to start with the following references. To which area of needs do these relate?

1. *Psalm 103:4*

2. *Matthew 6:33,34*

3. *Romans 5:8; 8:35,39*

4. *Ephesians 2:10*

Within this classification of needs the word *esteem* or *self-esteem* has arisen. This concept of self-esteem or self-image is one of the most important foundations of marriage. If one marries with a low self-esteem, a strain can be placed upon the marriage. You may have married in order to build your self-esteem or seeking to have your spouse give you a sense of meaning. (If you have questions about your worth, value, and feelings about yourself, you may want to read *Improving Your Self-image* by Norman Wright (Harvest House) and *The Sensation of Being Somebody* by Maurice Wagner (Zondervan).

Our self-image or self-concept is often built upon our appearance. We ask, "How do I look?" Is your self-concept built upon your appearance? It is also built upon the following. To what degree does your self-concept depend on each of these? Write your responses.

1. Status: "How important am I?"

2. Belongingness: being wanted or accepted

3. Worthiness: "I am good, I count."

4. Competence: feeling adequate

Let's look specifically at the last three. Belongingness rests on the voluntary attitude of others as they display their acceptance. It is a sense of security with others who love and accept you. Your spouse probably accepts you, but what happens during times when you feel a lack of acceptance? Worthiness rests on the introspective attitude of self-approval and being affirmed as a person of value. What happens when you don't feel that you approve of yourself? Competence rests on the evaluations received in past relationships and on one's present sense of success. What happens when you don't feel successful or when you're not?

Think about this: Your worth is so great that if you had been the only person created upon the earth, God still would have sent His son to die for you. You count that much to Him. Many of us strive for adequacy. God has declared us to be adequate in what He has done for us in His Son Jesus Christ.

In your relationship with God you are assured of belongingness. In your relationship with the Son of God you are assured of worthiness. In your relationship with the Holy Spirit you have a secure sense of competence as He is our Comforter, Guide, and Source of Strength. (If you would like more information about these concepts, please read the previously mentioned books.)

How will the presence of Jesus Christ in your life help you fulfill your needs and those of your spouse? How will His presence help you build your self-worth?

seven

Roles, Responsibilities, and Decision Making

What about the question of roles and responsibilities in marriage? Who does what and why? Does he or she do it? Is it because of tradition or because of what the church has said? Or is it because that is the way it was done in your parents' home?

Failure to clarify the husband-wife roles in a relationship is a major cause of marital disruption. As a couple you will be involved in an almost endless number of activities and responsibilities. Each couple should discuss together and decide who is most competent to do which task. Assignment of tasks should not be made simply because of parental example, because it is expected in your social group, or because of tradition. When an individual's abilities, training, and temperament make it difficult or unnecessary to follow an established cultural norm for a role, the couple will need to have the strength to establish their own style of working together. It is imperative that a couple deliberately and mutually develop the rules and guidelines for *their* relationship as husband and wife. This clear assignment of authority and responsibility by the spouses does not create a rigid relationship but allows flexibility and order in what could become a chaotic mess.

Let's spend some time now thinking about your role as a wife or husband.

"Woman's Place—Where Are You?"

Property—wife has almost no rights and privileges compared to those of the husband. Husband is the family provider. Often the wife is merely a chattel for the husband's sexual expression.

Complement—wife's rights have increased. Marriage is the wife's central life interest. Husband is chief provider and has more authority than wife. She is a friend to her husband. He achieves and she supports him.

Junior Partner—wife's rights increase because she works outside the home for pay. Her main motive is to improve the family's life-style. She has more authority (rights) than a nonworking woman.

Equal Partner—wife and husband share equal rights and responsibilities.

Property	Complement	Jr. Partner	Equal Partner

Place your answer on the chart with your initials and indicate what you feel your partner believes by placing his initials on the chart. When both of you have completed your chart, share your response.

Complete the following sentences and discuss them.

1. In marriage I believe a "role" is...

2. My main role in marriage is...

3. I began to form this belief about my role when...

4. My mate's role is...

5. In marriage a wife should...

6. In marriage a husband should...

7. I can best help my mate fulfill his or her role by...

Use a separate piece of paper for the Role Concepts Comparison which follows. Read each statement and write the appropriate number indicating what you believe about each one. Then go back and indicate how you think your partner responded to each statement. Finally, write for each one, where you obtained your belief—from your parents, pastor, friends, or your own idea.

YOUR ROLE CONCEPTS COMPARISON

What do you believe about your role concept in marriage? Circle:

(1) strongly agree

(2) mildly agree

(3) not sure

(4) mildly disagree

(5) strongly disagree

Wife		*Husband*
1 2 3 4 5	**A.** The husband is the head of the home.	1 2 3 4 5
1 2 3 4 5	**B.** The wife should not be employed outside the home.	1 2 3 4 5
1 2 3 4 5	**C.** The husband should help regularly with the dishes.	1 2 3 4 5
1 2 3 4 5	**D.** It is all right for the wife to initiate love-making with her husband.	1 2 3 4 5
1 2 3 4 5	**E.** The husband and wife should plan the budget and manage money matters together.	1 2 3 4 5
1 2 3 4 5	**F.** Neither the husband nor the wife should purchase an item costing more than $30 without consulting the other.	1 2 3 4 5
1 2 3 4 5	**G.** The father is the one responsible for disciplining the children.	1 2 3 4 5

Wife		Husband

Wife   **Husband**

1 2 3 4 5   **H.** A wife who has special talent should have a   1 2 3 4 5
career.

1 2 3 4 5   **I.** It is the wife's responsibility to keep the house   1 2 3 4 5
neat and clean.

1 2 3 4 5   **J.** The husband should take his wife out some-   1 2 3 4 5
where twice a month.

1 2 3 4 5   **K.** The wife is just as responsible for the chil-   1 2 3 4 5
dren's discipline as the husband.

1 2 3 4 5   **L.** It is the husband's job to do the yard work.   1 2 3 4 5

1 2 3 4 5   **M.** The mother should be the teacher of values to   1 2 3 4 5
the children.

1 2 3 4 5   **N.** Children should be allowed to help plan fami-   1 2 3 4 5
ly activities.

1 2 3 4 5   **O.** Children develop better in a home with par-   1 2 3 4 5
ents who are strict disciplinarians.

1 2 3 4 5   **P.** Money that the wife earns is her money.   1 2 3 4 5

1 2 3 4 5   **Q.** The husband should have at least one night a   1 2 3 4 5
week out with his friends.

1 2 3 4 5   **R.** The wife should always be the one to cook.   1 2 3 4 5

1 2 3 4 5   **S.** The husband's responsibility is to his job and   1 2 3 4 5
the wife's responsibility is to the home and
children.

What does the Word of God say concerning the role of the wife and the role of the husband? Read *Ephesians 5:21-33*.

1. What one word summarizes a wife's responsibility to her husband? Compare *1 Peter 3:1*.

2. What do the words "as unto the Lord" (v. 22) suggest about the wife's role?

3. Are there any limits placed upon the wife's submission by *Colossians 3:18* and *Acts 5:29*?

4. According to verse 33, what should the wife's attitude be toward her husband and what does this mean in *everyday life*?

5. What does the word "submission" mean to you? Write a definition.

It does not mean that she is inferior nor does it stifle her initiative. It does not limit her in any way. Read *Proverbs 31:10-31*. Make a list, on a separate piece of paper, of the ways this woman in Proverbs uses her abilities.

What is the man's role? Is submission ever part of his role and function? What does *Ephesians 5:21* say?

1. Study *Ephesians 5:22-33*. What two words in this section summarize the husband's responsibility? Compare verse *23* with verse *25*. See *Philippians 2:4*.

2. What example should the husband exhibit as he leads in the marriage relationship? Compare *Ephesians 5:23* with *1:22*. In light of this, for whose benefit should the headship of the husband be exercised?

3. For whose benefit is the headship of Christ exercised? Compare Ephesians *1:22* and *5:25-27*. In light of this, for whose benefit should the headship of the husband be exercised?

4. What are the ways in which Christ loved the church? Relate each of these to the way a husband should love his wife.

5. In Proverbs we see that the wife has been given great responsibility and is able to use her gifts. What gifts or ability does your wife have that you do not?

6. In *Proverbs 31:28,29*, the husband praises and expresses appreciation to his wife. Could it be that this is the reason that she is so capable?

Perhaps you are already getting the idea that in marriage each one gives to and receives from the other. Marriage is built upon each person being a complement to the other. Dr. Dwight Small expressed it in this way:

"When a man and a woman unite in marriage, humanity experiences a restoration to wholeness. The glory of the man is the acknowledgment that woman was created for him; the glory of the woman is the acknowledgment that man is incomplete without her. The humility of the woman is the acknowledgment that she was made for man; the humility of the man is the acknowledgment that he is incomplete without her. Both share an equal dignity, honor, and worth. Yes, and each shares a humility before the other, also. Each is necessarily the completion of the other; each is necessarily dependent upon the other." [10]

Earlier you probably discovered that the role of the husband is that of a servant. It is a servanthood role! What are some creative ways that a husband can be a loving leader-servant?

1.

2.

3.

4.

5.

6.

7.

8.

9.

10.

Decision Making

Who makes the decisions in the marital relationship? Perhaps the question is not who does or who should but who is best qualified. Who in the marital relationship exerts the most influence upon the other or carries more weight in deciding?

Use the following outline, following the instructions and writing your answers on a separate piece of paper. After both of you have done this, exchange papers, compare your answers, and discuss the results together.

One main question to consider is this: Does each of us make decisions in the areas where he or she is most gifted? Does each person have sufficient opportunity to give what he or she has to offer? What is the reason for one or the other having the percentage of influence that is evident?

Your Percentage of the Decision

Describe the decision-making process that you think you have in your marriage by putting the percentage of influence that you will have and that your spouse will have for various issues. The total for each decision must be 100 percent.

	Her Vote	His Vote
Choice of new car	———	———
Choice of home	———	———
Choice of furniture	———	———
Choice of your own wardrobe	———	———
Choice of vacation spots	———	———
Choice of decor for the home	———	———
Choice of mutual friends	———	———
Choice of entertainment	———	———
Choice of church	———	———
Choice of child-rearing practices	———	———
Choice of TV shows	———	———

Choice of home menu . . . . _____   _____

Choice of number of children . . . . _____   _____

Choice of where we live . . . . _____   _____

Choice of husband's vocation . . . . _____   _____

Choice of wife's vocation . . . . _____   _____

Choice of determining for what and how the money is spent . . . . _____   _____

Every couple directly or indirectly establishes a pattern for reaching marital decisions. Many of these patterns are ineffective or self-defeating. Some bring about lingering feelings of resentment. The majority of couples have not considered how they arrive at decisions.

1.   Who made most of the decisions in your family? How would your partner answer this question?

2.   Have you established guidelines to distinguish between major and minor decisions? If so, what are they?

3.   What procedure do you follow when there is an impasse and a decision must be made?

4.   How did you decide upon responsibilities for household chores?

5.   In what areas of family life do you have the right to make decisions without consulting your spouse? Who decided this policy and how did you arrive at this decision?

6.   Do you make the decisions that you want to make or the ones that your spouse does not want to make?

7.   Do you have any "veto power" over your spouse's decisions? If so, what is the basis for it and how did you arrive at this decision?

How did you do in answering these questions? Most couples have never thought them through, and yet they are vital to an understanding of the marital relationship.

Answer these questions and then compare your responses with those of your wife.

1.   I'm afraid to make decisions when...

2.   I'm afraid to have my partner make decisions when...

3.   I'd like to make decisions when...

4.   I'd like my partner to make decisions when...

5.   I want to make decisions in the area of...

6.   I want my partner to make decisions in the area of...

Consider these thoughts about the roles of the husband and wife and decision making:

"The principle of mutuality of submissiveness in marriage is similar to the pattern of submissiveness between the members of the Body of Christ. There are times in the Body when it is appropriate for one member to exercise leadership over the other members as a function of his or her spiritual gift (*1 Corinthians 12:14-26*). No single spiritual gift automatically qualifies a member to be the leader or ultimate decision maker all of the time. That position belongs to the head, Jesus Himself. Likewise in marriage, in which there is mutuality of submissiveness, the role of leadership is assigned not according to some decree from God, or on the basis of 'maleness' or 'femaleness,' but on the basis of the leadership role the partner has been assigned by the mutual decision of the marriage. The skill of a Christian marriage lies in the negotiation and assignment of these leadership roles on the basis of the abilities of the partners."[11]

"In the marriage the husband has the office of head. That simply means he has the responsibility and authority to call the marriage—his wife as well as himself—to obey the norm of troth. If he faithfully exercises his office, both he and his wife will be freed to be themselves. As the head, the husband is called to take the lead in mutually examining the marriage to see if it is developing according to its long-range goals.

"Clearly, headship has nothing to do with being boss. The husband can only command the wife to live up to what the two of them mutually pledged when they were married. Likewise, if the husband neglects his office, the wife ought to call the husband back to their mutual vows.

"Neither does headship imply inferiority or superiority. Rather, headship is a special office of service so that the marriage may thrive and grow. Headship does not mean that the husband leads or decides in every detail. Once a man and woman have decided which vision of life is going to norm their activities in their marriage, they can leave the decisions in day-to-day affairs to the partner with the appropriate talents, temperaments, and situations. The husband's role is to be on guard continually so that the 'little' things do not develop into the kinds of patterns that undermine the entire marriage."[12]

How will the presence of Jesus Christ in your life help you in the process of decision making and discovering your gifts in marriage?

eight

In-Laws or Outlaws— It's Your Choice

You are an in-law. What does the word *in-law* mean to you? Write your definition and share it with your partner.

What examples of in-laws do we find in the Scriptures? Read the following three selections and ask yourself, "How would I have responded if I had been in the same situation?"

1. *Genesis 26:34—27:46*

2. *Exodus 18:13-24*

3. *Ruth*

Describe the ideal in-law relationship from your perspective. Share this with your partner.

Describe what you think would be the ideal in-law relationship from your parents' perspective and from that of your partner's parents.

Remember the old quiz show on radio, "Twenty Questions"? Here are twenty of the most important questions concerning in-laws. Answer them, and then share your answers with your fiance.

1. *Genesis 2:24*; *Matthew 19:5*; *Mark 10:7,8*; and *Ephesians 5:31* all say the same thing. What does the word *leave* mean to you?

2. If your parents were to help you get started financially, what might they expect in return?

3. How do your parents feel about your marriage?

4. What emotional ties with your parents interfere with your relationship? Explain.

5. How do you think your in-laws view you?

6. What would you consider to be "interference" by your in-laws?

7. How did you get along with your mother and father during your childhood?

8. Describe your present relationship with your mother and father.

9. How do you think your parents view your partner?

10. What one thing about your partner's parents do you dislike?

11. What three things about your partner's parents do you really appreciate?

12. What customs in your home differ from those in your partner's home?

13. Describe how and where you like to spend your Thanksgiving and Christmas days.

14. What have you done in the past to let both your own parents and your in-laws know they are important to you?

15. During the past two weeks, what have you done to express your positive feelings toward your parents and your in-laws?

16. What new things could you say or do that would let your parents and your in-laws know they are important to you?

17. Describe what you have done to discover from your parents or in-laws what kind of relationship they expect from you and your partner. (Such as how often to visit or call, their involvement in disciplining children, etc.)

18. In the past how have you helped your parents or in-laws meet their own needs and develop a greater meaning in life?

How can you help them in the future?

19. In the past what have you done with your parents or in-laws to make it easier for them to demonstrate love toward you as a couple?

How can you improve this in the future?

20. What have you done in the past to assist your parents or in-laws to receive love from you? What have you done to demonstrate love to them?

If you would like additional information on the subject of in-laws, read *In-Laws, Outlaws: Building Better Relationships* by Norman Wright (Harvest House).

In what way will the presence of Jesus Christ in your life help you in building positive in-law relationships?

nine

Communication

Communication is to love what blood is to life. Have you ever thought about it in that way before? It is impossible to have any kind of relationship unless there is communication. That is true for you and your partner and for your relationship with God.

How would you define communication? What do you think the word means? Write your definition and then share your answer with your partner.

Now define *listening* and again share your definition.

At this point you may want to turn to the end of this section and read a definition of communication and a definition of listening. How important is communication? Think about this.

"If there is any indispensable insight with which a young married couple should begin their life together, it is that they should try to keep open, at all cost, the lines of communication between them."[13]

"A marriage can be likened to a large house with many rooms to which a couple fall heir on their wedding day. Their hope is to use and enjoy these rooms, as we do the rooms in a comfortable home, so that they will serve the many activities that make up their shared life. But in many marriages, doors are found to be locked—they represent areas in the relationship which the couple are unable to explore together. Attempts to open these doors lead to failure and frustration. The right key cannot be found. So the couple resign themselves to living together in only a few rooms that can be opened easily, leaving the rest of the house, with all its promising possibilities, unexplored and unused.

"There is, however, a master key that will open every door. It is not easy to find. Or, more correctly, it has to be forged by the couple together, and this can be very difficult. It is the great art of *effective marital communication*."[14]

Let's consider another aspect of communication. In our communication we send messages. Every message has three components: the actual content, the tone of voice, and the nonverbal communication. With changes in the tone of voice or in the nonverbal component, it is possible to express many different messages using the same word, statement, or question. Nonverbal communication includes facial expression, body posture, and actions. An example of nonverbal communication which should be avoided is holding a book in front of one's face while talking.

The three components of communication must be complementary. One researcher has suggested the following breakdown of the importance of the three components. [15] The percentages indicate how much of the message is sent through each one.

Content / 7%
Tone / 38%
Nonverbal / 55%

Confusing messages are often sent because the three components are contradicting one another.

Take a minute and think about how you communicate nonverbally. Then write how your partner communicates nonverbally. After you have done this, write what you think your nonverbal communication means to the other person and what you think your partner's nonverbal communication means. Ask your spouse to do this too, and then compare and discuss your responses.

Our nonverbal communication and tone of voice are essential elements in conveying our messages. If you are not aware of your tone of voice, you may want to use a tape recorder to record some of your conversations. Then play them back and pay attention to your tone of voice and what it implies.

How will you communicate in the following situations?

1. It's Saturday. Your spouse asks you to shop for something but you really don't want to go. You say:

2. You are trying to watch your favorite TV program but your spouse is continually interrupting and asking you questions. The program is at the crucial part and you don't want to miss it. You say:

3. You are describing to your spouse the most exciting event of the day. Right in the middle of it your spouse yawns and says, "I think I'll go get a cup of coffee." You say:

4. Your spouse serves you breakfast. You notice that the bacon is overcooked, which you don't like. The toast is served lightly toasted with fresh butter which is exactly what you like. You say:

5. After dinner your spouse asks you if you would do the dishes tonight since he or she is so tired. You, too, are tired and were looking forward to relaxing. Usually you both do them together. You say:

6. You have just had an argument with one of the children and you realize that you are wrong. It is not easy to apologize to family members because they usually rub it in. You say:

What does the Word of God say about communication? Look up the passages listed and write the key thought for each one. You will notice that the verses are listed in groupings as there is a central theme in each group. See if you can discover the central thought for each group and write it as a summary.

1. *Proverbs 11:9*
   Proverbs 12:18
   Proverbs 15:4
   Proverbs 18:8
   Proverbs 18:21
   Proverbs 25:11
   Proverbs 26:22
   James 3:8-10
   1 Peter 3:10

2. *Proverbs 4:20-23*
   Proverbs 6:12,14,18
   Proverbs 15:28
   Proverbs 16:2
   Proverbs 16:23

3. *Proverbs 15:31*
   Proverbs 18:13
   Proverbs 18:15
   Proverbs 19:20
   Proverbs 21:28
   James 1:19

4. *Proverbs 12:18*
   Proverbs 14:29
   Proverbs 15:28
   Proverbs 16:32
   Proverbs 21:23
   Proverbs 26:4
   Proverbs 29:20

5. *Proverbs 15:23*
   Proverbs 25:11

6. *Proverbs 10:19*
   Proverbs 11:12,13
   Proverbs 13:3
   Proverbs 17:27,28
   Proverbs 18:2
   Proverbs 20:19
   Proverbs 21:23

7. *Proverbs 17:9*
   Proverbs 21:9

8. *Proverbs 15:1*
   Proverbs 15:4
   Proverbs 16:1
   Proverbs 25:15

9. *Proverbs 12:16*
   Proverbs 19:11

10. *Proverbs 12:17,22*
    Proverbs 16:13
    Proverbs 19:5
    Proverbs 26:18,19
    Proverbs 26:22
    Proverbs 28:23
    Proverbs 29:5
    Ephesians 4:15,25
    Colossians 3:9

Let's see what kind of a communicator you are and discover how much you know about your wife. Assume that you are interviewing a stranger. Your task is to ask the other person any question you want about marriage, dating experiences, childhood, hobies, likes and dislikes, religious views, feelings about himself, his looks, etc. Keep in mind that you know nothing about the other person. Construct your questions so that you assume nothing. Keep your opinions out. When you have completed the interview, change roles and have your partner interview you.

In his book, *Why Am I Afraid to Tell You Who I Am?*, John Powell states that we communicate on five different levels, from shallow clichés to deep personal comments. Hang-ups, such as fear, apathy or a poor self-image keep us at the shallow level. If we can be freed from our restrictions, we can move to the deeper, more meaningful level.

The five levels of communication are:

Level Five: Cliché Conversation. This type of talk is very safe. We use phrases such as "How are you?" "How's the dog?" "Where have you been?" "I like your dress." In this type of conversation there is no personal sharing. Each person remains safely behind his defenses.

Level Four: Reporting the Facts about Others. In this kind of conversation we are content to tell others what someone else has said, but we offer no personal information on these facts. We report the facts like the six o'clock news. We share gossip and little narrations but we do not commit ourselves as to how we feel about it.

Level Three: My Ideas and Judgments. Real communication begins to unfold here. The person is willing to step out of his solitary confinement and risk telling some of his ideas and decisions. He is still cautious. If he senses that what he is saying is not being accepted, he will retreat.

Level Two: My Feelings or Emotions. At this level the person shares how he feels about facts, ideas, and judgments. His feelings underneath these areas are revealed. For a person to really share himself with another individual he must move to the level of sharing his feelings.

Level One: Complete Emotional and Personal Communication. All deep relationships must be based on absolute openness and honesty. This may be difficult to achieve because it involves risk—the risk of being rejected. But it is vital if relationships are to grow. There will be times when this type of communication is not as complete as it could be.[16]

Take the time right now and write down your answer to these questions:

1. What are some of the reasons why a person might respond only at level five or level four?

2. When do you feel most like responding at levels two and one?

3. At what level do you usually respond?

4. At what level does your partner usually respond?

5. On which level do you usually share with God?

6. Describe a time when you really felt that you communicated with God.

Persons who communicate primarily on a cognitive or thinking level deal mainly with factual data. They like to talk about such topics as sports, the stock market, money, houses, jobs, etc., keeping the subject of conversation out of the emotional area. Usually they are quite uncomfortable dealing with issues that elicit feelings, especially unpleasant feelings such as anger. Consequently they avoid talking about subjects that involve love, fear, and anger. These persons have difficulty, then, being warm and supportive of their spouses.

Others communicate more on the feeling level. They tire easily of purely factual data and feel a need to share feelings, especially with their spouses. They feel that the atmosphere between husband and wife must be as free as possible from unpleasant feelings like tension, anger, and resentment. So, of course, they want to talk about these emotional things, resolve conflicts with their spouse, clear the air, and keep things pleasant between them.

Of course no one is completely cognitive or completely emotional. Where are you and where is your wife? On the diagram below indicate (1) where you think you are, (2) where you think your fiance is, and (3) where you think your partner would place you.

Emotional   *Cognitive*

A person on the left side of the graph, who shares more feelings, is not less bright or less intellectual. This person is simply aware of his/her feelings and is usually better able to do something about them.

A surprising fact is that the so-called cognitive person (on the right) is controlled by his feelings just as is the so-called emotional person, but he doesn't realize it. For example, the stiff, formal intellectual has deep feelings also, but uses enormous energy to keep them buried so he won't be bothered with them. Unfortunately they do bother him. Whenever someone (like an ''emotional'' wife or child) is around asking him for affection and warmth, he is not only unable to respond, he is angered that his precious equilibrium has been disturbed.[17]

Communication is the process of sharing yourself, both verbally and nonverbally, in such a way that the other person can both accept and understand what you are sharing.

What is listening? Paul Tournier said, ''How beautiful, how grand and liberating this experience is, when people learn to help each other. It is impossible to overemphasize the immense need humans have to be really listened to. Listen to all the conversations of our world, between nations as well as those between couples. They are, for the most part, dialogues of the deaf.''[18]

The Living Bible expresses these thoughts about listening: ''Any story sounds true until someone tells the other side and sets the record straight'' (*Proverbs 18:17*). ''The wise man learns by listening; the simpleton can learn only by seeing scorners punished'' (*Proverbs 21:11*). ''He who answers a matter before he hears the facts, it is folly and shame to him'' (*Proverbs 18:13, Amplified*).

''Let every man be quick to hear, (a ready listener,)...'' (*James 1:19, Amplified*). What do we mean by listening? When we are listening to another person we are not thinking about what we are going to say when he stops talking. We are not busy formulating our response. We are concentrating on what is being said. Listening is also complete acceptance without judgement of what is said or how it is said. Often we fail to hear the message because we don't like the message or the tone of voice. We react and miss the meaning of what was being shared.

By acceptance, we do not mean that you have to agree with everything that is being said. Acceptance means that you understand that what the other person is saying is something he feels. Real listening means that we should be able to repeat what the other person has said and what we thought he was feeling when he was speaking to us.

It is important to become very proficient in communication. You may want to read *An Answer to Family Communication* by Norman Wright (Harvest House), and *Family Communication* by Sven Wahlroos (Macmillan).

ten

Conflict (or "Sound the Battle Cry!")

Are you anticipating conflict in your marriage? If not, you may be in for a surprise. Conflict is a fact of life. It has been defined as a slash, contention, or sharp disagreement over interests, ideas, etc. Why does it occur? The answer is simply that we are human beings—imperfect people whom God graciously loves in spite of our imperfection. Each of us has our own desires, wants, needs, and goals. Whenever any of these differ from another, conflict may occur. Our differences in beliefs, ideas, attitudes, feelings, and behavior will be different. The conflicts themselves are not the problem, but rather our reaction to them.

Many times disagreements or conflicts do not need to be completely resolved. An example may be a disagreement over political philosophy. This type of disagreement could continue indefinitely and need not destroy the overall marital relationship.

1. List some of the issues you and your partner disagree on that do not need to be completely resolved.

2. What does "completely resolved" mean to you?

3. Make a list of some issues on which you disagree that do need solutions—those on which more time needs to be spent exploring alternatives.

4. Select one of the issues on which more time needs to be spent. Write an explanation of the situation—as you see it.

5. Some people have learned to use weapons in dealing with conflict. What are some unfair weapons?

6. What effect does anger have upon a solution to conflict? What effect does anger have upon a marriage?

Remember that anger comes about for three basic reasons: hurt, fear, and frustration. (If you would like to explore this topic further, read *An Answer to Anger and Frustration* by Norman Wright (Harvest House).

What do the following verses have to say about the right way to handle anger?

1. *Psalm 37:1-11*

2. *Proverbs 14:29*

3. *Proverbs 15:1*

4. *Proverbs 15:28*

5. *Proverbs 16:32*

6. *Proverbs 19:11*

7. *Proverbs 25:28*

8. *Proverbs 29:11*

9. *Matthew 5:43,44*

10. *Romans 8:28,29*

11. *Romans 12:19,21*

12. *Galatians 5:16-23*

13. *Ephesians 4:26*

14. *Ephesians 4:29*

15. *Ephesians 4:32*

16. *1 Peter 3:9*

What causes conflicts? See James 4:1-3.

A look at your relationship:

1. Describe a recent or current conflict between you and your partner.

2. What do you believe caused the conflict? What was the outcome? What did it accomplish?

3. How did you create or contribute to the conflict?

4. Imagine that you are seeing the conflict from the other person's perspective. How would your partner describe the conflict?

5. If you could go through the same conflict again, how would you handle it?

Remember this: Conflict is a natural part of growth and family living. Many conflicts are simply symptoms of something else. Most people do not deal openly with conflict because no one has *ever* taught them effective ways of dealing with it. On the positive side, conflict does provide opportunity for growth in a relationship. Unresolved and buried conflicts arise from their grave and interfere with growth and satisfying relationships.

What choices do we have in dealing with conflicts? James Fairfield has suggested five styles of dealing with conflict.[19]

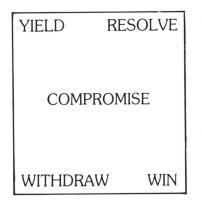

The first is to *withdraw*. If you have a tendency to view conflict as a hopeless inevitability which you can do little to control, you may not even try. You may withdraw physically by leaving the scene or you may leave psychologically.

If you feel that you must always look after your own interests or your self-concept is threatened in a conflict, you may choose to *win*. No matter what the cost, you must win! Domination is usually reflected in this style; personal relationships take second place.

While driving along the highway or approaching an intersection you have probably noticed a *yield* sign. "Giving in to get along" is another style. You don't like it, but rather than risk a confrontation you choose this path.

"Give a little to get a little" is called *compromise*. You may find that it is important to let up on some of your demands or ideas in order to help the other person give a little. You don't want to win all the time nor do you want the other person to win all the time.

A person may choose to *resolve* conflicts. In this style of dealing with conflicts, a situation, attitude, or behavior is changed by open and direct communication.

1. Select your usual style of dealing with conflicts.

2. Select your partner's usual style.

3. Describe a situation in which you withdrew from a conflict.

4. Describe a situation in which you won a conflict.

5. Describe a situation in which you yielded in a conflict.

6. Describe a situation in which you compromised in a conflict.

7. Describe a situation in which you resolved a conflict.

8. Describe how each solution affected the feelings of others toward you.

Withdrew:

Won:

Yielded:

Compromised:

Resolved:

9. How did you feel about yourself in each situation?

Withdrew:

Won:

Yielded:

Compromised:

Resolved:

10. Did the result eventually bring about a more peaceful atmosphere in each case?

What style did Jesus use? What styles of handling conflict do we find in the Scriptures? Take a few minutes and read the following accounts of conflict. Try to determine the methods used at that time. Write down the various styles you observe.

1. *Genesis 4*

2. *1 Samuel 20:30-34*

3. *Matthew 15:10-20*

4. *Mark 11:11-19*

5. *Luke 23:18-49*

6. *John 8:1-11*

7. *John 11:11-19*

You may ask, Which style is best? Which is best for our marriage?

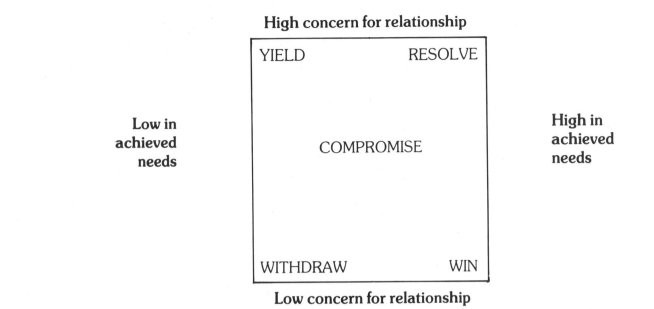

As you can see from the diagram above, *withdraw* has the lowest value because the person gives up on meeting the goals and developing the relationship. The relationship is turned off. If this style is used temporarily as a cooling off step toward *resolve*, it is beneficial. There may be times when the discussion is so heated and out of control that withdrawing is best. But it is important to make a definite and specific commitment to discuss and resolve the conflict.

The *win* method achieves the goal but can sacrifice the relationship. In a family, personal relationships are just as important or more important than the goal.

Yielding works just the other way in that the relationship is maintained but the goals are sacrificed.

Compromise attempts to work out some needs, but the bargaining involved may mean that you compromise some of your own values. If you have some basic convictions about the type of young men that your daughter dates and you begin to compromise your standards in order to have greater harmony, what does that do to you?

Naturally the highest value or style is *resolve* because in the final analysis relationships are strengthened as you seek to meet personal needs.

How then can we resolve conflicts? Consider trying and applying these principles:

1. When a conflict arises, instead of demanding that you be heard, listen carefully to the other person (see *Proverbs 18:13* and *James 1:19*). Any changes that one person wants to see in another must be heard and understood.

2. Select an appropriate time. ''A man has joy in making an apt answer, and a word spoken at the right moment, how good it is'' (Proverbs 15:23, *Amplified*).

3. Define the problem. How do you define the problem and how does the other person?

4. Define the areas of agreement and disagreement in the conflict.

5. Here comes the difficult part. A few conflicts *may* be just one-sided, but most involve contributions from both sides. Identify your own contribution to the problem. When you accept some responsibility for a problem, the other sees a willingness to cooperate and will probably be much more open to the discussion.

6. The next step is to state positively what behaviors on your part would probably help, and to be willing to ask for his opinion. As he shares with you, be open to his feelings, observations, and suggestions. Watch out for defensiveness!

Read the following passages in *The Living Bible*. What do these verses say?

1. *Proverbs 13:18*

2. *Proverbs 23:12*

3. *Proverbs 25:12*

4. *Proverbs 28:13*

How will the presence of Jesus Christ in your life help you deal with conflict?

eleven

Finances

Money! It takes money to eat, pay the rent, the tax collector, the grocer, etc. Your attitude toward money and past life style may have been an adjustment for you as you married. Financial disruption and difficulties in marriage can place a strain upon the marital relationship. The next several exercises have been designed to help you determine what is important to you in terms of finances and help you make some realistic plans.

First, let's see how aware you are of what items cost today.

"You paid *how much* for that?"

Secret thoughts of a husband: "I just can't understand why my wife is always short of money. Now if I took over, things would be more efficient and there would be money to spare."

A wife broods: "I don't know why my husband says he can't take me out more often. His expenses aren't that high."

Do you confess to thinking like that occasionally? Here is your chance to show how much you know about the day-to-day money problems your spouse faces. This quiz is divided into two sections, one for each partner. Each of you is asked to approximate the cost of 25 items or services that the other will probably pay for. Here are the rules:

Women ask their husbands the questions headed "For Men." Men ask their wives the questions headed "For Women." In some cases a price range rather than the approximate cost may be allowed.

Score four points for each correct answer. Don't be too strict. Give your spouse credit for a answer if he or she comes within, say, 10 percent of the right amount.

If you want to compare scores, go ahead. But that's not the point of the quiz. The idea is simply to show how well you understand your partner's side of the spending. And maybe the quiz will teach you a lesson: Don't beef about somebody's spending habits until you know what you are talking about.

For Men

How much would you
have to pay for these?

1. A 10-pound turkey _____
2. A five-pound bag of
   potatoes _____
3. A chocolate cake mix _____
4. A chuck roast for six _____
5. A week's supply of milk _____
6. A broom _____
7. A large box of detergent _____
8. A two-quart ceramic
   casserole with lid _____
9. A set of eight water
   glasses _____
10. A set of six steak knives _____
11. A fake fur coat _____
12. A pair of pantyhose _____
13. A three-piece polyester
    pants suit _____
14. A woman's swim suit _____
15. A girl's blouse _____
16. A pair of kid's jeans _____
17. A pair of children's
    shoes _____
18. A nylon lace half slip _____
19. A king-size no-iron sheet _____
20. A machine-washable, drip-
    dry tablecloth _____
21. 3½ yards of double-knit
    fabric _____
22. A pair of steel sewing
    shears _____
23. A pair of sheer Dacron
    window curtains _____
24. A permanent wave _____
25. A tube of lipstick _____

For Women

How much would you
have to pay for these?

1. A quart of motor oil _____
2. A chassis lubrication _____
3. A set of shock absorbers _____
4. A pair of first-line
   tires _____
5. A 20-inch power mower _____
6. Fertilizer to cover the
   lawn _____
7. A six-foot aluminum
   stepladder _____
8. A set of four screw-
   drivers _____
9. An adjustable wrench _____
10. A gallon of latex paint _____
11. A fiber glass fishing rod _____
12. A boy's baseball mitt _____
13. A haircut, including tip _____
14. The home heating bill
    for a year _____
15. The yearly federal
    income tax _____
16. Your husband's annual
    life insurance premiums _____
17. An ''off-the-rack''
    worsted suit _____
18. A man's raincoat _____
19. A medium-priced pair
    of shoes _____
20. A pair of knit slacks _____
21. A wash-and-wear shirt _____
22. Ten shares of American
    Tel & Tel _____
23. Dinner for four at a good
    restaurant, including tip _____
24. A businessman's lunch
    for two. _____
25. Two tickets to a football
    or baseball game _____

Study the following passages to discover how to acquire, how to regard, and how to spend money. Indicate the principles that you derive from each passage.

1. *Deuteronomy 8:17,18*

2. *1 Chronicles 29:11,12*

3. *Proverbs 11:24,25*

4. *Proverbs 11:28*

5. *Proverbs 12:10*

6. *Proverbs 13;11; 14:23*

7. *Proverbs 13:18, 22*

8. *Proverbs 15:6*

9. *Proverbs 15:16,17,22*

10. *Proverbs 15:27*

11. *Proverbs 16:8*

12. *Proverbs 16:16*

13. *Proverbs 20:4,14,18*

14. *Proverbs 21:5,6*

15. *Proverbs 21:20,25,26*

16. *Proverbs 22:1,4,7*

17. *Proverbs 23:1-5*

18. *Proverbs 24:30-34*

19. *Proverbs 27:23,24*

20. *Proverbs 28:6,22*

21. *Proverbs 30:24,25*

22. *Ecclesiastes 5:10*

23. *Ecclesiastes 5:19*

24. *Matthew 6:19,20*

25. *Matthew 17:24-27*

26. *Luke 6:27-38*

27. *Luke 12:13-21*

28. *Romans 13:6-8*

29. *Ephesians 4:28*

30. *Philippians 4:11-19*

31. *2 Thessalonians 3:7-12*

32. *1 Timothy 6:6-10*

33. *1 Timothy 6:17-19*

34. *Hebrews 13:5*

Dos and Don'ts for Budgeting

1. Plan together. Hold a definite date together—seek agreement and cooperation. Make decisions together. Figures and plans should be known by all.

2. Define your financial goals. Launch your budget with a purpose in mind. Have a clear idea of why you're trying to budget.

3. Don't rush into a budget before you know how much you now spend for what. Devote several weeks to keeping a detailed expense record for use in working on a budget. If you do not know where your money is going, you cannot sensibly decide where it should go.

4. Do not think up countless budget headings. Use common sense in approaching and clarifying and classifying according to your family's spending habits.

5. Divvy up your dollars according to the family's needs and wants. Do not allocate according to the way other people spend. Use averages, canned guides and other outside advice as rough starting points only. Indicate your specific needs and wants:

NEEDS	COST

WANTS	COST

6. Think first. When allocating, trimming or adjusting budget amounts, do not jump to conclusions. Do not let wishful thinking take the place of sober appraisal. Does an expense item look too high? Find out whether it really is high, or why it is high, before cutting it. If you are looking for a place to economize so you can spend more on something else, do not cut any old thing arbitrarily. Before you do whittle down an item, spell out precisely what specific items of past expenditures are to be reduced or eliminated.

7. Plan for the big expenses. You can expect several big, non-recurring expenses during the year—taxes, insurance, vacation bills, etc. Forecast, lay aside an amount each month to meet these expenses when they come due. If not planned for, a few of these dropped smack amidst regular, month-to-month expenses will throw your budget into chaos, from which it may never recover.

8. Know who is in charge of what. Each member of the family should know just what his or her responsibilities are.

9. Do not keep track of every penny. Each member in the family should be allowed to spend his allowance as he chooses, without having to make an entry in the budget. Do not insist that everyone keep itemized lists of all expenses. Do not demand detailed accounts and summaries.

10. Do not intermingle funds. Do have a clear-cut system for divvying up the paycheck. A checking account is a good system. You deposit a sum of money each payday to cover expenses, keeping record of how much is earmarked for what. This way you will not be spending more than you have allotted for any one budget item.

11. Do not cheat your budget. For example, do not misuse your charge account if your budgeting shows you cannot afford a new ski outfit this month. Do not go out and charge it. A debt like this should always be taken into account for next month's planning. Otherwise, you will find that a substantial amount of your funds has already been spent, thanks to the charge.

12. When the budget starts to rub tight, let it out here, tuck it in there, to give a better fit. Do not keep it ironclad and inflexible. A grim, unbending budget will soon make everybody sullen, if not outright mutinous. A good rule of evaluation is to look at your budget every January and every July to make certain that it is realistic and working for you to your benefit.

AND...do not quit at the first chance you get. Budgets seldom click the first time around. Hang on, start revising, try fresh starts. Do not toss in the towel. If at first you don't succeed, you know what to do!

As you make out your budget be sure to insert an item designated "Marriage Enrichment." This amount, which could be from $50 to $250 per year, is set aside for you to use for the enhancement of your marriage relationship. It can be used for books to read together, tapes to listen to together, honeymoon weekends, marriage enrichment retreats, etc. By doing this and planning this as a goal you should be able to build the quality of married life that you are both seeking at this time. But it doesn't just happen! It takes planning and work.

How will the presence of Jesus Christ in your life help you with the financial aspect of your married life?

Making the Budget Work

In making a budget work for you it is important that both partners decide and agree together, and be willing to be flexible. Also, there is nothing "sacred" that the man must "control" the purse strings. The most qualified partner should handle the finances, but remember, there needs to be *mutual agreement* on where the money goes.

Wes and Judy Roberts follow a very simple plan to direct the flow of their $$$. Like the vast majority of people there is the monthly struggle to make ends meet, and this is one plan which has helped them to achieve some financial goals they, at first, did not think were possible. This idea came from a book titled *How to Succeed with Your Money* by George Bowman (Moody Press) This formula is called the 10-70-20 Plan.

After taking out all of the taxes from your paycheck you are left with X amount of dollars. From that you also deduct your church tithe, pledge or offering. For the sake of simple illustration, let us say that your gross earnings are $1000, taxes amount to $200 and you are tithing $100. You are then left with $700 of useable income which is broken down in the following manner:

10% = $70 . . . . *Savings for investment for retirement* (never to be spent until retirement)

70% = $490 . . . .*For living expenses:*
housing (mortgage or rent)
food
insurance (car, health, etc.)
clothes
utilities (water, gas, phone, electricity, etc.)
car maintance (gas, repairs, etc.)
magazine subscriptions etc.

20% = $140 . . . . *To clear present debts* and accounts charging interest, then this can be used *to save for major purchases* (dishwasher, vacations, etc.) *and emergencies.*

Now, here is some space for you to figure out your own finances:

Gross earnings   _____

Subtract taxes and all withholding   _____

_____
Sub total

Subtract tithe, pledge or offering   _____

_____
Sub total— this is your useable income

10% of useable income: _____

70% of useable income: _____

20% of useable income: _____

In our society it is very easy to live beyond our income. Things are nice to have, but one of the biggest blessings you can experience in a marriage is living with a little less and living close to debt-free.

Savings are a must so invest that 10% for good returns and do not spend the money on anything but investments. Use the 70% to meet your living *needs* —it can be done! What you have left over, the 20%, you need to use to clear out those credit card charges then use this as an accumulating fund and pay cash for your wants even if it takes a little time to save up.

Read what Wes and Judy have to say: "A friend of ours from Corvallis, Oregon, first shared this with us soon after we were married, and we tried it from time to time. The times we tried were when we were getting far into debt. It worked to get us out of debt. Then we would

say, 'Oh, joy...look, some extra money!' And...boom....right back into debt we would go. Well, about the third time through this cycle we finally believed in the workability of this simple formula (it always got us out of debt). Now we are always saving something (10% of each paycheck after taxes and tithe), having what we need (70%, which is not always what we want, but definitely what we need), and, praise the Lord, we are staying out of debt (20%) and are able to get some of the things we want. If our earnings change we change the amounts, but the percentages stay the same. For us, this plan is terrific!''

BOOKS ABOUT PERSONAL FINANCE

Money Management Library
Published by: Money Management Institute
                 Household Finance Corporation
                 Prudential Plaza
                 Chicago, IL 60601

Christian Family Money Management and Financial Planning
Published by: Louis Neibauer Co., Inc.
                 Jenkintown, PA 19046

Handbook for Financial Faithfulness: A Scriptural Approach to Financial Planning
Published by: Zondervan Publishing House
                 1415 Lake Drive S.E.
                 Grand Rapids, MI. 49506

** *Your Finances in Changing Times: God's Principles for Managing Money*
Published by: Campus Crusade for Christ, Inc.

twelve

Sex in Marriage

Sex in marriage is supposed to grow and bloom into the best of intimate physical communication. And in some marriages "things"are getting better every day. But there are other marriages where sexual expressions (and not just intercourse) have become ruts of routine or non-existent. The Bible talks about four specific purposes for human sexual communication, and release. Look into what God's Word says about each of these purposes by reading the following Bible verses and talking over the discussion questions.

Procreation. Read *Genesis 1:28* and *Deuteronomy 7:13,14.* What evidence do these verses give that sexual activity for reproduction of the human race is part of God's design?

Read *Psalm 127:3* and *Psalm 139:13-15* from *The Living Bible.* What attitude toward human sexuality and reproduction do you discover in these verses?

Recreation and Release. Read *Song of Soloman 4:10-12* and *Proverbs 5:18,19.* Does it surprise or shock you that the Scriptures actually encourage the enjoyment and sensual delights of sex?

Reread *Proverbs 5:18,19,* remembering that the writer used poetic language as he spoke of sexual energies, drives, and outlets. Throughout the Bible a favorite symbol for sex is *water*—fountains, streams, cisterns, springs, wells, etc. Do you agree or disagree that *Proverbs 5:18,19* encourages a husband and wife to come to their bed to experience sexual pleasure? Write reasons why you agree or disagree here:

Communication. Read *Genesis 2:24.* Ideally, the "one flesh" spoken of in this verse means a blending of spirit, mind, soul—the entire being—with your spouse. Read the following paragraph that more fully describes the concept of "one flesh." Then answer the questions at the end of the paragraph.

In the plan of God, sex was intended to provide a means of totally revealing oneself to the beloved, of pouring one's energies and deepest affection, hopes, and dreams into the loved one. Sex provides a means of presenting one's spouse with the gift of oneself and experiencing a like gift in return; a means of saying, "I love you." In short, sex becomes a mode of communication, a means of "knowing" each other.

How do everyday experiences affect sexual closeness and communication? How can they affect a husband's or a wife's ability to give of oneself to the other?

1. What was the first question about sex that you can remember asking your parents? How did they respond?

2. From what source (parents, friends, books) did you first learn the basic facts (or rumors) about reproduction? Can you remember anything about how you felt when you received this information?

3. When you were growing up did you have anyone with whom you felt comfortable when talking about your questions concerning sex? Who was it? What made that person easy to talk with?

4. The word sex means...

5. In marriage sex is...

6. Agree or disagree: Men are "girl watchers"; women are not normally "man watchers."

7. How will you respond and deal with it if another person is attracted to you and approaches you?

8. What if you find yourself attracted to another person?

9. How important is sex in a Christian couple's marriage?

10. What difference would being a Christian make in a couple's sexual relationship in marriage?

Together, read this prayer, written by Harry Hollis, Jr., and then discuss how you felt about the content.

Lord, it's hard to know what sex really is—
Is it some demon put here to torment me?
Or some delicious seducer from reality?
It is neither of these, Lord.

I know what sex is—
    It is body and spirit,
    It is passion and tenderness,
    It is strong embrace and gentle hand-holding,
    It is open nakedness and hidden mystery,
    It is joyful tears on honeymoon faces, and
    It is tears on wrinkled faces at a golden
        wedding anniversary.

Sex is a quiet look across the room,
    A love note on a pillow,
    A rose laid on a breakfast plate,
    Laughter in the night.

Sex is life—not all of life—
    But wrapped up in the meaning of life.

Sex is your good gift, O God,
    To enrich life,
    To continue the race,

To communicate,
To show me who I am,
To reveal my mate,
To cleanse through "one flesh."

Lord, some people say
   Sex and religion don't mix;
But your Word says sex is good.
Help me to keep it good in my life.
Help me to be open about sex
   And still protect its mystery.
Help me to see that sex
   Is neither demon nor deity.
Help me not to climb into a fantasy world
   Of imaginary sexual partners;
Keep me in the real world
   To love the people you have created.

Teach me that my soul does not have to
      frown at sex
   For me to be a Christian.

It's hard for many people to say,
   "Thank God for sex!"
Because for them sex is more a problem
   Than a gift.
They need to know that sex and gospel
Can be linked together again.
They need to hear the good news about sex.
Show me how I can help them.

Thank you, Lord, for making me a sexual being.
Thank you for showing me how to treat others
   with trust and love.
Thank you for letting me talk to you about sex.
Thank you that I feel free to say:
   "Thank God for sex!"

[From Harry Hollis, Jr., *Thank God for Sex*
(Nashville: Broadman Press, 1975), pp. 11-12]

A Description of Our Sexual Experience

Initiation
What kind of things tend to stimulate you sexually (get you "turned on")?

Describe a typical process of initiation of sexual intercourse for you and your spouse (who does what, how does the other respond, etc.).

What about the process of initiation in your sexual relationship would you like to change?

Pleasuring

What kind of sexual stimulation by your partner is most pleasurable for you? Describe the kind of touch, places, length of time, etc.

Where in your body do you feel the most intense sexual sensations during sexual pleasuring?

Describe your feelings during this phase of a typical sexual experience for you and your spouse (includes the process of bringing your worlds together, entry, and enjoying the process).

Responding—"Letting Go"

Describe what the sensations of sexual release are like for you. If you do not experience sexual release, try to describe at what point your feelings start to wane and what happens then.

Relaxing—Affirming

What do you usually do and feel during this time?

What do you sense from your partner at this time?

How might you be more affirming to your partner during the relaxation phase?

The material in this section of sexuality is simply an introduction. It is very important that you be fully informed of both the physiological and biblical facts concerning sex. The vast majority of individuals are not nearly as informed as they could be, and surprisingly enough women are more informed in most cases than men. It would be most beneficial to listen to the cassette series *Sex Problems and Sex Techniques in Marriage* by Dr. Ed Wheat, a Christian medical doctor. In addition, the book entitled *Solomon on Sex,* by James Dillow, is an excellent presentation, both on the teachings of the Song of Solomon and practical suggestions on romance in marriage. (Both of these can be ordered from your bookstore or from Christian Marriage Enrichment, 8000 E. Girard, Denver, CO 80231. The tape series is $13.95 and the book is $7.95. Send prepaid with $.35 per each item for postage and handling.)

References

1. Sydney Smith, *Lady Holland's Memoir,* Vol. I (London: Longman, Brown, Green & Longman, 1855).

2. David Augsburger, *Cherishable: Love and Marriage* (Scottdale, PA: Herald Press, 1971), p. 16.

3. From Elton Trueblood. Source unknown.

4. Daniel Freeman, "Why Get Married?" *Theology News and Notes of Fuller Theological Seminary,* 1973 (December 1973, 19:4), p. 17.

5. From a message by Dr. David Hubbard, President of Fuller Theological Seminary.

6. Ira J. Tanner, *Loneliness: The Fear of Love* (New York: Harper & Row, 1973), pp. 92,93.

7. Abraham Schmitt, *Conflict and Ecstacy— Model for a Maturing Marriage.* From an original paper by the author.

8. James G. T. Fairfield, *When You Don't Agree: A Guide to Resolving Marriage and Family Conflict* (Scottdale, PA: Herald Press, 1977), p. 195.

9. Paul Welter, *Family Problems and Predicaments* (Wheaton, IL: Tyndale House, 1977), p. 101.

10. Dwight H. Small, *Christian: Celebrate Your Sexuality* (Old Tappan, NJ: Revell, 1974), p. 144.

11. Dennis Guernsey, *Thoroughly Married* (Waco, TX: Word Books, 1976), p. 70.

12. James Olthuis, *I Pledge Thee My Troth* (New York: Harper & Row, 1975), p. 27.

13. Reuel Howe, *Herein Is Love* (Valley Forge, PA: Judson Press, 1961), p. 100.

14. David and Vera Mace, *We Can Have Better Marriages If We Really Want Them* (Nashville, TN: Abingdon Press, 1974).

15. Albert Metowbian, *Silent Messages* (Belmont, CA: Wadsworth Publishing Company, 1971), pp. 42-44.

16. Adapted from John Powell, *Why Am I Afraid to Tell You Who I Am?* (Niles, IL: Argus Communications, 1969), pp. 54-62.

17. Ross Campbell, *How to Really Love Your Child* (Wheaton, IL: Victor Books, 1977), p. 20.

18. Paul Tournier, *To Understand Each Other* (Richmond, VA: John Knox Press, 1967), p. 29.

19. James Fairfield, *When You Don't Agree* (Herald Press), pp. 33,34,231.

Your
Wedding Ceremony

What did you want your
wedding ceremony to represent?
What did you want it to say to you,
to those in attendance, and to God?
Take time right now and describe the
wedding vows you made.
Can you remember?

EVALUATION FORM FOR "AFTER YOU SAY 'I DO'"

Age _____ Sex _____

How long have you been married? _____

Is this a first marriage for you? _____

What was most helpful to you in this series? Topic, discussion, etc.?

_____

_____

What specific changes have you made because of this instruction?

_____

_____

_____

What specific changes have you seen in your spouse because of this series?

_____

_____

_____

What will you do to continue to enrich your marriage?

_____

_____

_____

_____

_____

_____

In what way could this series be improved?

_____

_____

_____

_____

Thank you for assisting us in this way. Please mail this form to:

Christian Marriage Enrichment
17821 17th Street, Suite 290
Tustin, California 92680